THE LITTLE BOOK OF
BALANCE

Parts of this book were first published in 2020 by Trigger, an imprint of Shaw Callaghan Ltd.

This expanded edition published in 2023 by OH! an Imprint of Welbeck Non-Fiction Limited, part of Welbeck Publishing Group. Offices in: London – 20 Mortimer Street, London W1T 3JW and Sydney – 205 Commonwealth Street, Surry Hills 2010 www.welbeckpublishing.com

Compilation text © Welbeck Non-Fiction Limited 2023 Design © Welbeck Non-Fiction Limited 2023

Disclaimer:

ISBN 978-1-80069-352-4

Editorial: Victoria Denne
Project manager: Russell Porter
Production: Jess Brisley

A CIP catalogue record for this book is available from the British Library

Printed in China

10 9 8 7 6 5 4 3 2 1

THE LITTLE BOOK OF

BALANCE

FOR WHEN LIFE
GETS A LITTLE TOUGH

CONTENTS

INTRODUCTION .- 6

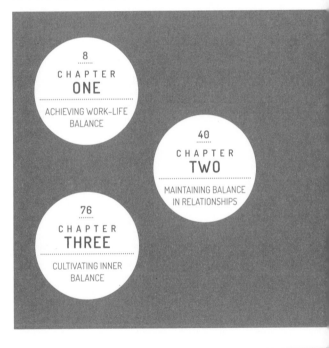

8

CHAPTER
ONE

ACHIEVING WORK-LIFE
BALANCE

40

CHAPTER
TWO

MAINTAINING BALANCE
IN RELATIONSHIPS

76

CHAPTER
THREE

CULTIVATING INNER
BALANCE

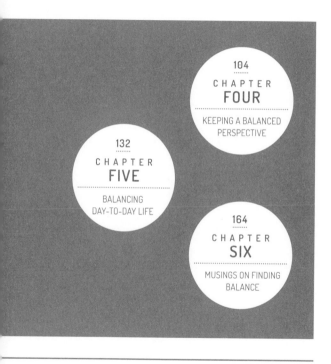

104

CHAPTER
FOUR

KEEPING A BALANCED
PERSPECTIVE

132

CHAPTER
FIVE

BALANCING
DAY-TO-DAY LIFE

164

CHAPTER
SIX

MUSINGS ON FINDING
BALANCE

INTRODUCTION

Life is a continual balancing act, and often the more we pursue balance, the more things seem to fall apart. All aspects of life – career, family, relationships, and health and wellbeing – are in perpetual motion, and it's this constant state of flux that makes it hard for us to attend to them in equal measure.

The Little Book of Balance offers guidance from some of the world's greatest minds in the art of letting each aspect of life feed off each other equally. To lead a well-balanced life, we must first accept that balance isn't something we can control.

CHAPTER

1

ACHIEVING WORK–LIFE BALANCE

Balancing a career with family life, relationships and social commitments is often challenging, yet it's essential in order to achieve a sense of happiness and fulfilment in life as a whole.

"

Balancing on a rope requires skill, steady feet, a steady mind and a sense of weight control. As you can see, the act of balancing consists of several things. Some of these things may be small but at the same time necessary to put the act together. A lot of people find it hard to balance work.

Ginel Love

Our lives are a mixture of different roles. Most of us are doing the best we can to find whatever the right balance is ... For me, that balance is family, work, and service.

Hillary Rodham Clinton

Never get so busy making a living
that you forget to make a life.

Dolly Parton

I don't like the word 'juggling' or 'work–life balance'. You prioritize.

Joanna Coles

Having time for everything that's important to me makes me feel very balanced, relaxed, and optimistic.

Steve Pavlina

66

When we refuse to balance the overwhelming demands of work, home, family, friends, and personal growth, stress will be the natural result.

Mary Southerland

66

Live a balanced life – learn some
and think some and draw and paint
and sing and dance and play and
work every day some.

Robert Fulghum

66

Many of us are trying to balance work, home, and a family life. We tend not to accept the early symptoms of burnout and carry on our daily lives. In my opinion, living your life isn't supposed to be that way. If you ignore the red flags, you'll become gravely ill, and your life could come to a complete halt.

Yasmeen Abdur-Rahman

You can't do a good job
if your job is all you do.

Katie Thurmes

When you have balance in your life, work becomes an entirely different experience. There is a passion that moves you to a whole new level of fulfilment and gratitude, and that's when you can do your best for yourself and for others.

Cara Delevingne

"

I think if I manage to juggle a personal life that I'm really happy with as well, as long as I manage to maintain balance, that's kind of the mark of success to me.

Rose McIver

There will always be another email to get through; something to clean up, file, and organize; more errands to do. Which is why balance is so important. Life is a marathon, not a sprint.

Gretchen Butler

"

Balance in general is difficult, but I refuse to go through life and just have work and not have good balance. I want to be an example, not only to my own children but

also to artists and other entrepreneurs,
that you can be a workaholic and also be
a good husband and good father.

Scooter Braun

66

You want to strike that happy medium:
the balance of being able to find creative
satisfaction in your profession, be able to
afford a roof over your head, but still have
the freedom to live a relatively normal life.

Chris Evans

"

I feel like I needed a balance. I don't
want to forget about my personal life
and spending time with myself.

Brandy Norwood

66

A 'harmonized' life these days
sounds like a tall order. Between
housework, homework, workwork,
and busywork, there are perpetually
too many things to do, and not
enough time to find that mythical

balance. Nothing is more frustrating than feeling like you're doing doing doing but getting nothing truly done that you really want.

Jack Canfield

Everything is about balance.
You can't work, work, work, work
without any play.

Janelle Monáe

Focus on being balanced –
success is balance.

Laila Ali

"

I love what I do for a living – it's the greatest job in the world – but you have to survive an awful lot of attention that you don't truly deserve, and you have to live up to your professional responsibilities, and I'm always trying to balance that with what is really important.

Tom Hanks

> If somebody tells you that he or she doesn't procrastinate, it's a lie. In small doses, it can be even helpful. If you don't take a pause from time to time, you can burn out very quickly.

Zoe McKay

"

Balance is a feeling derived from being whole and complete; it's a sense of harmony. It is essential to maintaining quality in life and work.

Joshua Orange

66

I like work/life separation, not work/
life balance. What I mean
by that is, if I'm on, I want to be on
and maximally productive. If I'm off,
I don't want to think about work.

When people strive for work/life balance, they end up blending them. That's how you end up checking email all day Saturday.

Tim Ferriss

You think you're getting sick this time
every year because you over-schedule for
the weeks leading up to Christmas and
then you miraculously recover and vow to
have a greater work–life balance.

Kayley Loring

Work–life balance is not an entitlement
or benefit. Your company cannot give it to
you. You have to create it for yourself.

Matthew Kelly

CHAPTER

2

MAINTAINING BALANCE IN RELATIONSHIPS

A balanced relationship is a healthy relationship. Recognizing the natural ebb and flow of any relationship is essential to ensure that both parties feel comfortable and supported.

"

You should learn to live a balanced life while overcoming problems and accepting each other's strength and weaknesses.

Adam Green

66

I'm a believer in the parent first,
friend second philosophy, and trying
to find that balance.

Jenna Fischer

66

What I tell my kids is, 'I'm preparing you for college and for life. So, having independence, knowing how to set your own boundaries, figuring out how to make that balance.

Michelle Obama

While it is important to love others unselfishly, it is crucial to find a balance. When we compromise our needs and martyr ourselves to the point of depleting ourselves and neglecting our needs, we become out of balance.

Jessica Minty

“

Women need real moments
of solitude and self-reflection
to balance out how much
of ourselves we give away.

Barbara De Angelis

"

My theme is, 'The spirit of friendship is the balance of life.' Not money. Not the World Series. It's friendship. The relationships I have with people, that's enough to keep me happy.

Ernie Banks

Letting go helps us to live in a more peaceful state of mind and helps restore our balance. It allows others to be responsible for themselves and for us to take our hands off situations that do not belong to us. This frees us from unnecessary stress.

Melody Beattie

Life is all about balance. My work
is very important to me, but so are
my relationships. I make time for that
aspect of my life, and it makes me
happy having balance in my life.

Samantha Barks

The mother who understands her own intentions and her daughter's intentions, who has introspection and a strong sense of self, and who is able to separate her identity from her daughter's, has the key to achieving the right balance.

Susan Shapiro Barash

Balanced relationships are always
based in freedom, not obligation.

Michael Thomas Sunnarbor

In a relationship, prudent application of the grey theory is a key ingredient in assuring years of happiness; 'till death do us part'. Balance is at the centre of success, satisfaction and a lifetime of love.

Carlos Wallace

> Don't just be a taker; healthy relationships require balance. Give with your words and be extra generous with your deeds.

Steve Maraboli

Countless mistakes in marriage, parenting, ministry, and other relationships are failures to balance grace and truth. Sometimes we neglect both. Often we choose one over the other.

Randy Alcorn

Being judgmental is a form of attack keeping others off balance.

David W. Earle

Marriage, in my view, should
be a balanced stalemate between
equal adversaries.

Elizabeth Peters

"

One of the most beautiful qualities
of true friendship is to understand
and to be understood.

Lucius Annaeus Seneca

Only equals make friends.
Every other relationship is
contrived and off-balance.

Maya Angelou

66

A good relationship is all about
balance and chemistry.

Taylor Swift

"

One reason I practice meditation
is to maintain my own balance and
clarity of mind in the face of such
huge challenges, and to be able to
stay more or less on course through

all the weather changes that, as a parent, I encounter day in and day out on this journey.

Myla and Jon Kabat-Zinn

66

As parents we often struggle with balancing our desire to make our children happy and setting boundaries.

Ellen Trump

If we are stressed out, we won't
be 'joyful mothers of children.'
Balance is key.

Katherine Leigh

"

What most people don't realize
is that marriage is a union of not only
to people in regard to the ceremony,
the tradition, but also the legality of
being married, but also interacting

with this other human being in a way that is going to bring balance to both of your lives.

Cathy Pearson

10 Ways to Maintain Balance in a Relationship

1. Communication
2. Respect your partner's privacy
3. Accept disagreement
4. Respect your partner's wishes
5. Build trust
6. Commit, but don't compromise much
7. Don't be too dependent on your partner
8. Figure out your relationship attributes
9. Be true to yourself
10. Consider each other in decision-making

Source: marriage.com

Relationship is about forgiveness and compromise. It is about balance where one person compliments each other.

Nicholas Sparks

"

Regardless of the gender of the highest wage earner, the balance of power in the relationship will suffer if the higher earner uses control of the purse strings as a system of reward and punishment. It will also suffer if the lower earner takes a chippy, haughty attitude to spending money they haven't actually generated themselves.

Marian Keyes

In long-term relationships ...
we are called upon to navigate
that delicate balance between
separateness and connectedness ...

we confront the challenge
of sustaining both – without
losing either.

Harriet Lerner

In marriage, compromise
nurtures the relationship.

Tim Allen

A relationship should be a
balance between two people.
One person shouldn't be giving,
while the other is only taking.

Unknown

Good boundaries, created by the use of good intimacy skills, keep a committed or intimate relationship lightly balanced between the needs of the individual and the needs of the relationship.

Anne Katherine

66

Your relationships with others are always a direct reflection of the relationship you have with yourself.

Michael Thomas Sunnarborg

CHAPTER

3

CULTIVATING INNER BALANCE

A continuous practice that requires us to follow our senses, cultivating inner balance involves supporting sustainable, healthy behaviours and allowing for internal healing.

"

To talk about balance, it's easier to talk about what's out of balance. And I think anytime that you have any disease, and disease meaning lack of ease, lack of flow ... dis-ease. So any

time there's disease, you're out of
balance, whether it's jealousy, anger,
greed, anxiety, fear.

Ricky Williams

66

Self-care is, fundamentally, about bringing balance back to a life that has grown imbalanced from too many commitments or responsibilities.

Robyn L. Gobin

A good method of juggling different tasks is to always balance the short- and long-term tasks.

Gretchen Pilar

The people that I admire
have a wonderful balance of
self-belief and humility.

Mahershala Ali

I do find that there's a fine balance between preparation and seeing what happens naturally.

Timothee Chalamet

"

When it comes to balance, you have
been sold a bill of goods. It's time to
give yourself a break, embrace the
life you have, and make adjustments
that will allow you to grow in the

areas that are crucial to your
most important commitments as
well as your happiness.

Dan Thurmon

66

Self-esteem is a matter of
balance. Too much can tip over
into haughtiness, arrogance, and
the inability to admit when we
have gone wrong.

Alan Schmidt

We are all tasked to balance
and optimize ourselves.

Mae Jemison

66

Take some time to learn which opinions you need to value and which ones you simply need to stop listening to. Once you find

the balance, you are one step
closer to finding that confidence
that you long for.

Frankie Robinson

Happiness is not a matter of
intensity but of balance and order
and rhythm and harmony.

Thomas Merton

> When you can, it's good to make healthy choices. But, I also believe in balance. It's not about being 100% this way or that way. It's about making healthy choices when you can.

Miranda Kerr

I've learned that you can't have everything and do everything at the same time.

Oprah Winfrey

I think recharging is important,
absolutely. Every now and then,
you need maybe a couple of weeks
to just chill out and let your emotions
balance themselves out a little bit.

Malin Akerman

"

One should see the world, and
see himself as a scale with an
equal balance of good and evil.
When he does one good deed
the scale is tipped to the good

– he and the world is saved.
When he does one evil deed the
scale is tipped to the bad – he and
the world is destroyed.

Maimonides

66

The body needs its rest, and sleep
is extremely important in any health
regimen. There should be three main
things: eating, exercise and sleep.
All three together in the right balance
make for a truly healthy lifestyle.

Rohit Shetty

Getting in balance is not so much about adopting new strategies to change your behaviours, as it is about realigning yourself in all of your thoughts so as to create a balance between what you desire and how you conduct your life on a daily basis.

Wayne Dyer

"

In this life, we are in a constant
search for inner peace. We long for
it in all aspects of our lives, both
personally and professionally. The
truth is that we cannot have inner

peace without balance. It seems that having too much or too little of anything completely throws off our balance, therefore limiting our inner peace.

Raheem DeVaughn

"

We benefit, intellectually and
personally, from the interplay
between the different selves, from
the balance between long-term
contemplation and short-term
impulse. We should be wary

about tipping the scales too far.
The community of selves shouldn't be
a democracy, but it shouldn't
be a dictatorship, either.

Paul Bloom

"

When you feel sad, it's okay. It's not
the end of the world. Everyone has
those days when you doubt yourself,
and when you feel like everything you

do sucks, but then there's those days when you feel like Superman. It's just the balance of the world.

Mac Miller

CHAPTER
4

KEEPING A BALANCED PERSPECTIVE

Recognizing imbalance is essential to maintaining a balanced perspective. This in turn enables us to better manage passionate emotional responses to challenging circumstances.

66

Living a balanced life is not about being in control of all things, but rather, about managing those things over which we do have an influence and managing our reaction to everything else.

Michael Hinz

"

If you look around, balance can be found everywhere. This is how the world is made and continues to sustain itself. If there are men, there are women. If there is day, there is night. It is all about balance.

Laurie Cain

The foundation stones for a
balanced success are honesty,
character, integrity, faith,
love and loyalty.

Zig Ziglar

There's a balance to be sought
between being too much involved
and not involved enough.

Mark Hodgson

Wisdom is your perspective on life, your sense of balance, your understanding of how the various parts and principles apply and relate to each other.

Steven R. Covey

Balanced is not better time management, but better boundary management. Balanced means making choices and enjoying those choices.

Betsy Jacobson

66

If you align expectations with reality,
you will never be disappointed.

Terrell Owens

"

Overcome your barriers, intend
the best, and be patient. You will
enjoy more balance, more growth,
more income, and more fun.

Jack Canfield

The hardest thing to find in life is balance – especially the more success you have, the more you look to the other side of the gate. What do I need to stay grounded, in touch, in love, connected, emotionally balanced? Look within yourself.

Celine Dion

66

I surround myself with positive,
happy people. And I always try to
balance things that I have to do
with things that I want to do.

Nina Agdai

For me it's important to be in balance. To not let fear get in the way of things, to not worry so much about protecting yourself all the time.

John Frusciante

Life is like riding a bicycle.
To keep your balance,
you must keep moving.

Albert Einstein

Our lives are a mixture of different roles. Most of us are doing the best we can to find whatever the right balance is. For me, that balance is family, work, and service.

Hillary Rodham Clinton

66

You can't start with imbalance
and end with peace, be that in
your own body, in an ecosystem or
between a government

and its people. What we need
to strive for is not perfection,
but balance.

Ani DiFranco

“

Time and balance: the two most
difficult things to have control over,
yet they are both the things that
we do control.

Catherine Pulsifer

I'm not suggesting you deny or suppress your emotions, but just discover for yourself what it takes for you to handle your emotions and stay balanced.

Wendy Hearn

66

A well-developed sense of humour
is the pole that adds balance to your
step as you walk the tightrope of life.

William A. Ward

66

Through substitute activities, therapy,
and hard work, grieving individuals
can work through their anger and
progress to live more balanced lives.

Valerie Orr

Your beliefs should knock the scale way off-balance leaning to the side of love. If the other side is weighed down with worry, guilt, shame, anger or frustration, choose right now to change that!

Debbie Dixon

66

There is no limit to what great and
beautiful things the human being can
create with the power of a balanced mind
that is open to the inspiration of God.

Paul Odafe Akpomukai

"

As time progresses, increase the
amount of time spent for self-
improvement, and less time on the
mental junk food. Create a healthy

balance, it's no different than indulging in some cake here and there. Moderation, moderation, moderation!

Curt Hinson

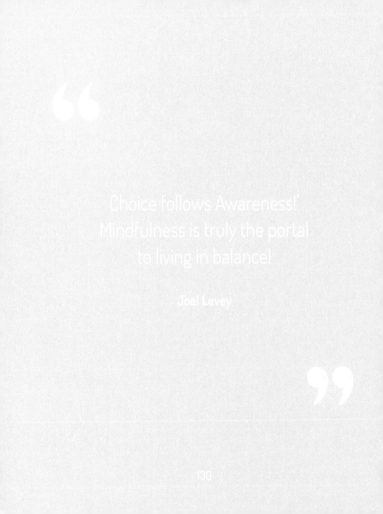

"

Choice follows Awareness!
Mindfulness is truly the portal
to living in balance!

Joel Levey

"

66

Understand that building self-confidence is all about striking a balance in your life. The right amount of confidence can help a great deal in achieving what you want.

Angel Graff

CHAPTER
5

BALANCING DAY-TO-DAY LIFE

Taking steps to achieve a healthy life balance facilitates better focus on attaining goals, taking productive actions, and making meaningful changes.

Do not take life too seriously.
You will never get out of it alive.

Elbert Hubbard

You will never find time for anything.
If you want time, you must make it.

Charles Buxton

"

Like with anything in life, find
the balance between too much
work and being too lazy; between
spending too much and being a
scrooge between being gone all the

time and being in each other's way;
between talking each other's ears
off and dead silence.

Christian Olsen

"

Balance is good, because one
extreme or the other leads to misery,
and I've spent a lot of my life at one
of those extremes.

Trent Reznor

Live a life that is well balanced;
don't do things in excess.

Daniel Smith

66

Our culture doesn't always promote balance. Instead, we want everything instantly, and we are willing to pay a premium later. We're impatient.

Jeff Kooz

There is no such thing as perfect, and balance will look different from person to person.

Rachel Dresdale

When we put balance to
work in each area of our lives,
we truly experience greater
balance, greater reward.

Jeff Kooz

A well-developed sense of humour
is the pole that adds balance to your
steps as you walk the tightrope of life.

William Arthur Ward

66

If you focus on negative and put out negative every day, the scales of life are off-balance the only thing that can return is the

negative, you added no positive
to the scale to balance.

B. W. Robertson

The best and safest thing is to keep a
balance in your life, acknowledge the
great powers around us and in us.
If you can do that, and live that way,
you are really a wise man.

Euripedes

"

In fact, everyone should take time
out once in a while to recharge
and revitalize their energy. The key
is to have a balanced life.

Michael Lee

Perfection ruins the balance
of life. People wish for zero
sadness, zero death, zero
illness, and zero challenge.

If all these 'bad' things are removed, what are we going to live for?

Russell Davis

"

It's really important to have
balance, spend some time in
nature, go to a few parties, enjoy
my friends and really chill out.

Joakim Noah

Everything in moderation, and
there's a perfect balance in this
life if we can find it.

Ryan Robbins

Life is about balance, and we
all have to make the effort in
areas that we can to enable us to
make a difference.

Orlando Bloom

The trick to balance is to not
make sacrificing important
things become the norm.

Simon Sinek

In life, there's a yin and a yang
and a balance. And when you don't
have balance, you have comedy.

George Lopez

It's about having an active lifestyle, staying healthy, and making the right decisions. Life is about balance.

Apolo Ohno

“

I think health is the outcome
of finding a balance and some
satisfaction at the table.

Alice Waters

Health is a state of complete
harmony of the body, mind and
spirit. When one is free from physical
disabilities and mental distractions,
the gates of the soul open.

B. K. S. Iyengar

66

Too much of one thing can end up creating stress; this is something that no one needs in their life. But living a life in balance can provide harmony and peace.

Catherine Pulsifer

Balance is not something you find;
it's something you create.

Jana Kingsford

Pursuing your goal is in a sense,
fired by internal motivation.
Hence, you need a source of
external motivation to keep
things in balance.

Ben Robinson

Balance is reached by realizing
that each moment is a spiritual
experience, and every action
is an expression of your
spiritual consciousness.

Eliott James

"

The secret to living a balanced
life mentally, physically, spiritually,
and socially boils down to one
thing — PRIORITIES.

Joy Clary Brown

66

In life when things get shaky and
we are trying to get our balance, we
need to fall back on what we know
to be true and follow the principles that
help us to live the life we desire.

Andrew Farland

CHAPTER

6

MUSINGS ON FINDING BALANCE

When it comes to finding balance, don't approach it with a perfectionist mentality. Balance is not a destination but a continual journey of self-discovery.

I was a little, uh, incorrigible as a kid, so the kitchen was a good place to give me structure and balance. It taught me hard work, but then I grew to love it.

Aaron Sanchez

There is no decision that we can make
that doesn't come with some sort of
balance or sacrifice.

Simon Sinek

The creative people I admire seem
to share many characteristics:
a fierce restlessness. Healthy
cynicism. A real world perspective.
An ability to simplify. Restraint.

Patience. A genuine balance of confidence and insecurity. And most important, humanity.

David Droga

Balance isn't something
you achieve 'someday'.

Nick Vujicic

Beauty is only skin deep. I think
what's really important is finding
a balance of mind, body and spirit.

Jennifer Lopez

"

Serenity is the balance between good and bad, life and death, horrors and pleasures. Life is, as it were, defined by death. If there wasn't death of things, then there wouldn't be any life to celebrate.

Norman Davies

"

We all strive for balance, often moving to extremes to find ourselves somewhere in the middle where we can sustainably exist in optimal inspiration. Working toward balance takes a lot of ingredients. We need courage, reflection, attention, action, and a push-and-pull relationship between effort and relaxation.

Tara Stiles

Doubt can motivate you, so don't
be afraid of it. Confidence and
doubt are at two ends of the
scale, and you need both.
They balance each other out.

Barbra Streisand

Balance is key: I need to be successful
in my career to feel fulfilled, be
surrounded by people I care about to
share it with, and have my health to
be able to do the things I love to do!

Kiana Tom

66

You have to find balance. Whenever
I start feeling stressed or not feeling
myself, it's about balance, and it means
I need to find it again.

Bernard Sumner

I always try to balance the light with the heavy – a few tears of human spirit in with the sequins and the fringes.

Bette Midler

"

I learned a few years ago that
balance is the key to a happy and
successful life, and a huge part of
achieving that balance is to instil
rituals into your everyday life.

A nutritious balanced diet, daily exercise, time for yourself through meditation, reading, journaling, yoga, daily reflection, and setting goals.

Gretchen Bieller

"

Because there is no cosmic
point to the life that each of us
perceives on this distant bit of
dust at the galaxy's edge ... there
is all the more reason for us to
maintain in proper balance what

we have here. Because there is nothing else. No thing. This is it. And quite enough, all in all.

Gore Vidal

66

Any time you start judging with
an overly critical eye rather than
letting things just be and following
what you think is right, it's
complicated to find balance.

Juliette Lewis

The delicate balance of
mentoring someone is not
creating them in your own
image, but giving them
the opportunity to
create themselves.

Steven Spielberg

66

Balance takes work. Lots of it. There is no endpoint in balance, no goal, no finalization. Balance requires practice, patience, and – most importantly –

movement. We often get stuck in our ways and form habits based on our fears and driven by our insecurities.

Tara Stiles

"

Everyone's goals are the same
with very small differences. I mean,
the goal of a socialist and the goal
of a libertarian are exactly the

same. The goals are happiness
and security and freedom, and
you balance those.

Penn Jillette

66

What I dream of is an art of
balance, of purity and serenity
devoid of troubling or depressing
subject matter – a soothing,
calming influence of the mind,

rather like a good armchair
which provides relaxation from
physical fatigue.

Henri Matisse

Balanced thinking will take
you beyond confusion.

Daphne Michaels